THE

WEEPING WILLOW,

BY

MRS. L. H. SIGOURNEY.

"Willows by the water-courses."
ISAIAH.

"Weeping may endure for a night,
But joy cometh in the morning."
DAVID.

HARTFORD.
HENRY S. PARSONS.
1847.

STEREOTYPED BY
RICHARD H. HOBBS,
HARTFORD, CONN.

TO

DANIEL WADSWORTH, Esq.

THE FRIEND

OF ALL WHO MOURN;

THIS LITTLE BOOK IS DEDICATED

WITH THE

GRATITUDE AND RESPECT

OF

THE AUTHOR.

CONTENTS.

PREFACE.

THE poems in this volume, as its title indicates, are adapted to those who have felt the pain of bereavement. A portion of them owe their birth to sympathy with passing sorrows, and have, as it were, been baptized with the mourner's tear. An increasing desire among those who endure the sundering of affection's ties for some simple lyric, fashioned to their own peculiar wound, marks our state of society, and, perhaps, the age in which we live.

There is often with deep grief, a hallowed jealousy. It seeks to be alone, that it may meditate without interruption, on the loved and lost. The voice of even the dearest, may inadvertently touch some chord, whose vibration is anguish. It may chance to inflict a pang, when it would shed a balsam. So, that the silence of the friends of Job is felt to be the truest wisdom; and a quiet mingling of tears, the safest sympathy.

Over this season of solitude, perchance too long or too gloomily cherished, the sigh of sacred poesy steals without startling. Culling the blessed words of Scripture, she lays them, like dewy flowers, in the lap of the weeper, and departs. But a soothing melody is left behind, as sweet as the breath of the buds that she brought,

> "While many a holy text around she strews
> To teach the mournful moralist *to die*,"

perhaps, also, the still harder lesson, *to live*, when what made existence lovely, is gone—to return no more.

It has been said, the friendships that take root in affliction have peculiar vitality and fervor. Their office and ministry of consolation supply all deficiencies in date, giving them the force of an attachment that time had tested.

Therefore, to those who mourn, may this, my little book, come with such a friendship, loving them better because they have wept,—pointing through the shade of the willow boughs where their harp is hung, to the "clear shining of the sun of righteousness," and breathing a prayer that this "light affliction, which is but for a moment, may work out a far more exceeding and eternal weight of glory."

L. H. S.

HARTFORD, November 2nd, 1846.

THE WEEPING WILLOW.

THE PASSING BELL.

OH! solemn passing bell
What said thy measured knell
  In ancient time?*
When for the listening throng,
Borne by life's tide along,
A pause in Folly's song
  Made the low chime.

Slowly, o'er rock and dell,
Thus thy deep accents fell,
  Thus spake the toll:
"One of thine own frail race
Gaspeth in Death's embrace,
  Pray for his soul.

"The strong man's arm is weak,
See from pale brow and cheek

---

* In ancient times the passing bell was tolled when a fellow-being approached death, that Christians might unite in supplication for a peaceful passage to the departing soul. This usage was probably abolished about the time of the Reformation.

Cold dewdrops roll;
How can he break away
From those who need his stay?
Pray for the soul.

"Hark! to a wailing sound,
A household gather round
With grief and dole,
The mother struggleth sore,
She heeds her babe no more,
Pray for her soul.

"To Beauty's shaded room
The Spoiler's step of gloom
Hath darkly stole,
Her lips are ghastly white,
A film is o'er her sight,
Pray for the soul."

Oh bell, that slowly toll'd!
Were these thy words of old,
Bidding men bow
In prayer for those who bear
The pang they soon must share?
What say'st thou now?

"One from his dear abode
Travelleth the churchyard road
To his last bed,
The widow next the bier
Walketh, with blinding tear,
Toll for the dead.

"The pauper layeth down
Gaunt Penury's galling crown

Of scorn and dread,
Great as a king he goes
Unto his long repose,
Toll for the dead.

"From crib and cradle fair,
From Love's unresting care
A child hath fled,
Let snowdrops lift their eye
Where that shorn bud must lie,
Toll for the dead.

"Low 'neath the coffin lid
The aged one hath hid
His hoary head,
On staff, at sunny door,
You 'll see him lean no more,
Toll for the dead."

Oh, holy passing bell!
Mingling thy mournful knell
Thus with our tears,
While like the shuttle's flight,
Like the short summer night,
Fleet our brief years;

Prompt us His will to do,
Bid us His favor sue,
Warn us His wrath to rue,
Unto whose eye,
Unto whose bar of dread,
Judge of the quick and dead,
Every hour's silent tread
Bringeth us nigh.

THE VOICE OF FAITH.

THE wife, from whom the heart of love
  Its highest solace drew,
The mother, circled by the plants
  That in her shadow grew,
Why, from the climax of her joys
  At vigorous noon she fell,
The eye of Reason cannot see,
  The voice of Faith can tell.

The Christian, who her Master's cross
  With saintly meekness bare,
Who for the sad and needy toil'd
  With pity's tireless care,
Why, smitten from her shining course
  She sleeps in lowly cell,
The eye of Reason cannot see,
  The voice of Faith can tell.

The rapture of the saintly soul
  That walk'd with God below,
When rais'd above the sway of sin,
  Above the sting of woe,
Where bloom the everlasting bowers,
  Where songs of angels swell,
The mortal heart hath ne'er conceived,
  The voice of Faith can tell.

THE SON OF THE WIDOW.

"The only son of his mother, and she a widow."

He languished by the wayside, and fell down
Before the noon-day. In his hand were flowers
Pledg'd to his lady-love. They died with him,
Like her young joys.
There was a widow'd form,
To whom the echo of his coming step
Had been as music. Now, alone she sits,
Tearful and pale. The world, henceforth, to her,
Is desolate and void.
Young love may weep,
But sunbeams dry its tears, and the quick pulse
Of hope, in beauty's bosom, overcomes
The syncope of grief.
But unto Age,
So utterly bereav'd,—what more remains,
Save with bow'd head, and finger on its lip
In silent meekness, and in sanctity,
The heavenly pilot ever in its view,
To pass the narrow, storm-swoln strait that bars
Time from Eternity.

THE ORPHAN'S SECOND BIRTH-DAY.

THE birth-day feast in thought was spread,
And Fancy smil'd to see
The orphan with her fairy tread
So full of merry glee,
'Mid the sweet group of infant friends,
Essay the playful wile,
Exulting, clap her tiny hands,
And wear her mother's smile.

The birth-day came! The change, how great!
Fast fell the mourner's tear,
The gourd had wither'd in a night,
The banquet was not here;
No! no! the banquet was above,
At the Redeemer's feet,
The cherub in its parents' arms,
And every bliss complete.

THE PARTING AND RETURNING BRIDE.

FROM her father's home, in her beauty's bloom
  Went forth the youthful bride—
A holy smile on her trusting brow,
  And her lov'd one by her side.

Though fair was that home, in its vernal pride,
  Yet brief was the parting tear,
For the arm of the chosen was round her thrown,
  And his voice to her heart was dear.

So another dwelling she fondly wreath'd
  With the charm of a woman's love,
With the hope that doth bud in the secret heart,
  And the faith that hath fruit above.

Once more to her father's gate she came,
  To the wealth of her native vale,
The holy smile on her brow the same,
  But that brow like a lily pale.

No word to the longing ear she spake,
  She sooth'd not the friend who wept,
For on her arm was a pallid babe,
  And the same deep sleep they slept.

They made them a bed in the churchyard green
  Ere the autumn leaf was sere,
And the riven turf as it droop'd that day
  Was damp with the mourners' tear.

Yet gain'd they not as a gift of love,
  A glimpse thro' the crystal sky,
Of the bride and her babe in the bliss above,
  Where the beautiful cannot die?

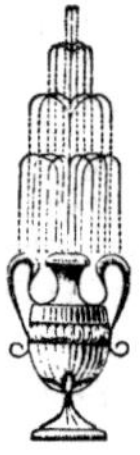

SOWN IN WEAKNESS.

"Sown in weakness, and raised in power."
ST. PAUL.

We've sown a precious seed,
That in our hearts was nurs'd,
A germ that promis'd fairest bloom,
We've sown it in the dust,
And darkly o'er our joys
There fell a withering blight,
As higher rose the swelling mound,
That hid it from our sight.

We sow'd it, while the winds
Were sweeping wild and wide,
While Winter struck the leafless trees,
And hollow groans replied;
Yet strength was in our souls,
Though griev'd and tempest-tost,
For by a Saviour's word of truth,
We knew it was not lost.

Not lost! though buried deep
Beneath the frozen plain,
We trusted that the vernal breath
Would give it life again;
Not that capricious beam
Which clouds so often shade,
But yon Eternal Spring, that wakes
The flowers that never fade.

ANNIVERSARY OF THE DEATH OF AN AGED FRIEND.

Again o'er time's receding track,
Unfaded comes thine image back,
Oh thou ! in childhood's years my pride,
Of joyous youth, the friend and guide
Thy form, by hoary age unbent,
Thy hand, on generous deeds intent,
Gleam o'er my eye, illusion dear !
And freshly wake the parting tear.

Tho' on this well-remember'd day
When thou didst sink to lowly clay,
Thy distant tomb I may not see
Nor bid one flower to bloom for thee,
Nor musing there, at evening's fall
Thy lessons to my soul recall,
It matters not ; for hovering nigh
Thy living accents seem to sigh,
Thy voice to breathe the sacred song,
Thy love to make my spirit strong,
And while such balm thou still dost shed,
I scarce can feel that thou art dead.

As from thy lips when life was new;
The lore of heavenly peace I drew,
And o'er thy coffin, bending low,
First conn'd the alphabet of woe,

So. changeless in my bosom's cell
The memory of thy love shall dwell,
And still my prayer invoke the sky
Like thee to live; like thee to die.

THE PERFECTED UNION.

The world is poorer when just souls depart,
They leave it darkened.
Faithful Spring remands
From wintry wastes her buried treasures back,
And bids the drooping shrub and leafless tree
Again replenish their collapsing veins
With fresh life-blood.
But the warm, beating heart
Of human sympathy, the mind enriched
With stores of knowledge, won by studious toil,
The noble form that tower'd in manhood's grace,
These, from the tomb return to earth no more—
No more.
The wandering bird may find again
Her long-forsaken nest, and wildly pour
The accustom'd strain; but man's unconscious ear,
That lingering listen'd to the melody,
Heeds not the carol from its sepulchre.

Yet thou for whom we mourn, art gather'd *home*;
The gentle hand of Love did beckon thee
To blest society. Thou heard'st a voice
In thy lone chamber, that we might not hear,
Wooing thee upward. So, thy step was swift
In the bright pathway of that bosom friend

Who knew no higher joy than o'er thy heart
To throw a shield from earth's adversity,
Or with the magic of the Eolian harp,
Transform the blast to music.
Now her watch
O'er thee is ended; and though we lament
No more to greet thee, with thy chasten'd smile,
Clear-minded, eloquent in speech and thought,
And full of zeal for truth; yet well we know
Thou art at rest with her.
'T is well with both.

THE LAST OF THE SEVEN.

Written on seeing a lifeless infant in its cradle.

It held a heather in its hand,
Its mother's favorite flower,
The native plant of Scotia's hills.
And dear Edina's bower,

And meekly in its snowy hand
White rose-buds droop'd the head,
As there, in peaceful sleep it lay
Upon its cradle-bed.

A line of coral mark'd its lip,
A smile, its forehead clear,
But not the changeful smile of those
Who have their wakening here.

No, no! Its welcome was above,
Sisters and brothers fair
Have clasp'd it in their arms of love
For all the seven are there.

The seven are there, and tears no more
Disturb their sweet repose,
In infant innocence they fell,
To heavenly bliss they rose:

And we, who feel how sins and cares
Earth's lingering pilgrim stain,
Give joy to that united band,
On yon celestial plain.

THOUGHTS AT THE COMMUNION.

WHERE are they, who by our side
Knelt, remembering Jesus died?
Drank with us, the cup he shed?
Shar'd with us, the broken bread?
Taught us, with their radiant eye,
How to live and how to die?

Are they not where none hath seen
Faded lip or mournful mien,
Brow with mortal sickness pale,
Locks that bleach, or limbs that fail,
Feet in darken'd paths that stray,
Hearts that yield to sorrow's sway?

List! to music soft and clear,
Angels answer, "*they are here!*"
Though we daily weep to miss
Trusting word, or tender kiss;
Though the home no more is bright,
Whence they took their seraph flight;
Father! Thou who know'st our pain,
Still, we bless Thee for their gain.

THE STUDENT AT COLLEGE.

THE lov'd of many a heart, went forth
In life's unclouded hour,
And bade his pleasant home adieu
For Learning's classic bower;
No lingering sadness dimm'd his eye,
Though all he left was dear,
For youthful ardor kindling high
Exhal'd the transient tear.

But knows the warbler of the air
That skims the flowery plain,
If all unscath'd by shaft or snare
He greet his nest again?
And man, for whom the foe and thorn
In ceaseless ambush wait,
Ill may the rosy lips of morn
Predict his evening fate.

Oh mother! gird thy bursting heart
A lifeless form to see,
And yield thine idol back to Him
Who lent the boon to thee.
And father! in thy manly strength
The wildering pang restrain,
And soothe thy children's grief for him
Who ne'er returns again.

For what, alas! were earthly Love,
  So often veil'd in gloom,
Look'd not her tearful eye above
  The tempest and the tomb,
Grasp'd not her hand a pledge divine
  Beyond this clime of pain,
Her scatter'd pearls once more to join
  In Heaven's unbroken chain.

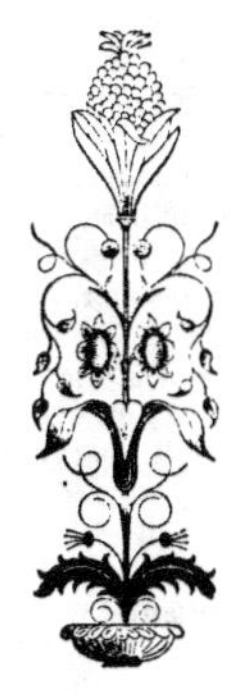

FUNERAL OF A FRIEND.

Not for the seal on the dark, lustrous eye,
The rigor settling o'er the beauteous brow
Wrapp'd in the richness of its raven hair
Lament too much: for lo! the unyielding grave,
That over-gorged. and watchful creditor,
Doth claim them by its bond and covenant
Of "dust to dust." And it shall render back
A glorious body, for the lifeless germ
Sown in its sterile soil, this day, with tears.

But for the loss of her sweet intercourse,
Who made the charities of home so dear
To wearied manhood, and confiding child,
And welcome guest, who o'er each duty cast
Such winning charm of perfect loveliness,
As made even trials, ministers of grace,
Whose love to her Redeemer, and the Book
Of inspiration, and the hallow'd courts
Of sacred worship, gave a brighter zest
To all the joys of youth; for such a loss
Lament and weep. It is the privilege
Of the chastised.

Yet be ye also fill'd
With priceless memories of gratitude,
As those who with an angel walk'd below,
And felt the influence of her speaking smile
Still luring heavenward, and beheld her spread,
As in the twinkling of an eye, the wing
That bore a ready spirit home, to God.

EARTH'S TREASURES.

"All perish with the using."
ST. PAUL.

THE sparkling eye that rul'd the heart,
  Hath lost its magic beam,
And in its socket heavily
  Like waning lamp doth gleam.
The wearied ear remits its toil,
  Rejects the music strain,
And with the folly of the world
  No longer loads the brain.

The hand, that with untiring deeds
  Did mark the days of old,
Now trembleth in its feeble grasp
  The water-cup to hold.
The foot no more o'er hill and dale
  Doth keep its vigorous way,
But on the cushioned sofa rests,
  A prisoner, day by day.

Dim Memory, with a wrinkled brow,
  Is faltering o'er the page
On which she register'd her gains,
  From infancy to age.
Even Fancy faileth in her skill
  O'er fairy-land to soar,
And sadly folds a broken wing,
  To ride the blast no more.

Yet the sweet spirit's love to man,
  In God its fearless trust,
Its zeal to keep a Saviour's law,
  These fade not in the dust,
These perish not with use, but grow
  Like beaten gold more bright,
The deathless children of the skies,
  That heavenward take their flight.

THE PEACE OF THE CHRISTIAN.

"See! in what peace a Christian *can die*."
ADDISON.

CAN joy exist, where anguish reigns?
Sweet peace, 'mid nature's fiercest pains?
A triumph-strain, when every tie
Is rent in mortal agony?

Oh, thou, who doubt'st if this may be,
Approach yon curtain'd couch, and see.

Behold a form, whose youthful morn
Hath known no cloud, whose rose no thorn,
Whose bosom's love no cruel blight,
Whose fondest hope no chilling night,
Still, on her brow, the bridal wreath
Is glittering in the grasp of death,
Hark! from her lips the victor lay
Doth warble, as she sinks away,
And o'er her pallid cheek, the while,
Doth gleam that dear Redeemer's smile,
The quick to hear, the strong to save,
His hand she clasps and dares the wave.

No dimness quells her spirit's light,
Her fearless faith is turn'd to sight,
And welcom'd by celestial bands
Safe on the eternal shore she stands.

But ye who mourn with ceaseless tear
The absence of a friend so dear,—
Who find inscrib'd on all below,
A want, a weariness, a woe,
Look up! her home of bliss survey
The pole-star of your pilgrim-way,
Grave on your hearts her parting strain,
And heed her charge "*to meet again.*"

DEATH OF A YOUNG MAIDEN.

SHE sleepeth on the shroud, on her white bed,
Amid the weepers. There was none to say
" *Talitha cumi,*" or uplift the head
That in its flood of auburn tresses lay,

Scarcely dishevel'd: With so slight a pain
The dark-rob'd Angel waved his fearful rod,
And from the beauteous clay that knew no stain
Drew forth the pure in heart, to see her God.

Repine not at her honor, ye who train'd
For highest excellence the child so dear,
Repine not that the perfect fruit is gain'd
Of all your plantings, all your waterings here:

But firmer tread this thorn-encumber'd sod,
Ennobled by your gift,—a seraph sent to God.

THE FAITHFUL EDITOR.

At thine own fireside, is the sob of grief,
And from yon distant hearth, that mother's moan
Who reap'd a blessed harvest in her age
From thy fond, filial love.
Those too, there are,
In many a region of our wide-spread land,
Who held communion with thee, week by week,
While years swept on, through thine unfolded scroll
Of pleasant knowledge, wing'd with tireless zeal
O'er hill and dale,— even where the settler builds
His cabin on the wild.
They mourn thy loss,
For Friendship quickeneth and may grow uncheer'd
By sight of feature, or by sound of voice,
Linking their thoughts together, whom the world
Conning her note-book of formalities,
Pronounceth strangers.
Thou didst wisely feel
How great their charge, who feed the public mind,
And with a high and heaven-taught spirit strive
To neutralize the poison that corrodes
Its health, and with an appetite for truth
Replace the gilded trifles that impair
Its nerve and firmness.

Thousands give thee thanks
Who never saw thy face. And so, farewell,
Kind heart, and true.
The good that thou hast done,
Shall blossom in men's souls when thou art gone,
And when the stem that bore it shriveleth,
Its essence shall go up and meet thee where
Its root can never die.

THE WIDOW'S DAUGHTER.

Tears for the beautiful!—who sank
  From life's scarce-tasted cup away,
As fades the lily on its stalk,
  As fleets the dewdrop from the spray.

Tears for the widow'd mother's gem!
  On which her trembling trust was staid,
Snatch'd from her desolated breast,
  And in the earth's cold casket laid.

Joy for the fragile form!—released
  From sharp disease and sleepless pain,
That drank the fount of being dry,
  And made affection's anguish vain.

Joy for the ransom'd soul!—at rest
  With Him, to whom it early gave
Its vows,—who crush'd the spoiler's sting,
  And took the victory from the grave.

For thus our faith, with mystic power
  Elicits praise from sorrow's sigh,
And from the blended tear and smile
  Compoundeth incense for the sky.

THE FALLEN ROSE.

A Rose was gather'd from the bower,
  Where lovingly it grew,
By summer's genial sunbeam cheer'd
  And fed with dew.

Who pluck'd it from its home away?
  A thoughtless passer-by?
A vengeful heart on evil bent?
  An envious eye?

Who broke the stalk? Methought a voice
  Spake tenderly and low,
"No careless hand this deed hath wrought,
  No cruel foe:

The florist, who the plant had rear'd,
  Set on the flower his seal,
He sows the seed to reap the fruit,
  He wounds to heal."

OUR OLDEST MAN.

MEEK patriarch of our city,—art thou dead?
  The just, the saintly and the full of days,
The crown of ripen'd wisdom on thy head,
  The poor man's blessing, and the good man's
    praise?
Would that our sons, who saw thee onward move
  With step unfailing, and serenely sage,
Of thee might learn to practice, and to love
  The hardy virtues of an earlier age.

For more than four-score winters had not chill'd
  The glow of healthful years, on lip, or cheek,
Nor in thy breast the warm pulsation still'd
  That moves with upright zeal to act and speak.
Ne'er from the righteous cause withheld by fear,
  Neither of toil ashamed, nor proud of wealth,
But trained in habits simple and sincere,
  From whence republics draw their vital health.

To every kind affection gently true,
  The husband, and the father, and the friend,
Thy children's children still delighted drew
  Around the honor'd grandsire's chair to bend.

But now thy mansion hath its master lost,
  Rich in its pleasant green, with trees o'erspread,
And we, a patriot sire, who knew the cost
  Of blood-bought freedom, in the day of dread.

We mourn thee, patriarch! On thy staff no more
  Thy cheerful smile shall greet us, day by day,
Nor the far memories of thy treasur'd lore,
  Withhold the joyous list'ners from their play.
Where stood the men of old, we fear to stand,
  In foremost watch on life's beleaguer'd wall,
To bide the battle with a feebler hand,
  Perchance to falter, and perchance to fall.

Oh God of Strength!—who takest from our head,
  The white haired fathers, firm in faith and truth,
Grant us thy grace, to follow where they led,
  A pure example to observant youth,
That tho' the sea of time should fiercely roll,
  We so its billows and its waves may stem,
As not to lose the sunshine of the soul,
  Nor our eternal rest in Heaven, with them.

THE MOTHER'S PARTING GIFT.

"Come near, my little ones," the Mother said,
And by her side they stood, two gentle forms,
In infant innocence, with earnest look,
While her emaciate hand, some treasure drew,
From 'neath the pillow.
"Take my parting gift,
Heaven's blessed book, dear babes.
When ye are skill'd
To read its pages, love them for my sake;
And every morn and even, pray to Him
The Almighty Father, who will be your guide
When I am gone. For he was still the stay
Of my lone orphanage, and all my life
Hath led me tenderly. And so, good night!
Go, sleep, my darlings."
Much they wonder'd why
Dear Mother in such feeble whisper spake,
Pausing so oft, and why her hollow cheek
Grew marble pale. Again she bade them go
To their sweet rest, for o'er her boding soul
The sable Angel hover'd; and she knew
Her struggle must be strong with him that night,
Nor would she have their tender spirits griev'd
At the fierce anguish.

Side by side they lay
In rosy dream, hand interlock'd in hand,
And clustering curls commingled.
Thick the shafts
Of agony, in the death-chamber fell,
And the flesh wrestled, and the spirit prayed
Till break of day.
Yet still, when morning came,
Breath stirr'd the sufferer's bosom, and once more
The brother with his little sister stood
Beside the sufferer's couch. Her bloodless lip
Press'd one long kiss upon their polish'd brow,
As with strange lustre gleaming from the eye,
The last, fond sunbeam of maternal love
Ere it became seraphic,—the freed soul
Leaping the bondage of all earthly ties
Went up with hallelujah.

ON THE DEATH OF A LADY.

WITH tranquil brow of holy ray
To pass from all we love, away,
To find like gathering mists unroll'd
Beneath the morning's glance of gold,
That chilling fear of death dispell'd
Which erst the soul in bondage held,
Are gifts vouchsaf'd to few who bear
This pilgrim-lot of pain and care.

Yet were they thine,—for whom o'erflow
This day, affection's tears of woe.
Thine! who by shafts of sorrow tried
Still clinging to thy Saviour-guide,
Sat at His feet, with constant heart,
Intent to choose that "better part."

I see thee still, with beaming eye,
As when bright Summer last swept by,
Thy form of grace, thy features fair
With beauty age could ne'er impair,
Arranging in thy snowy vase,
Rich breathing flowers, with matchless grace,
Or bidding tireless bounties flow
At pallid penury's tale of woe.

But now, thy happy home no more
Can be, what it hath been before,

To child, to friend, to favour'd guest,
To wanderer sad, to soul distress'd,
Its cherish'd plants must fade away,
The woodbine round its porch decay,
Its lamp withhold the diamond spark,
Its pleasant halls be lone and dark ;
Yet thou,—who o'er the wreck of time,
Hast gain'd a mansion more sublime,
Lend us thy light, o'er thorns to tread,
Lend us thy smile, when hope hath fled,
That when on our last couch we rest,
With swimming eye and fainting breast,
A lesson we may teach, like thee,
Of the blest spirit's victory.

THE YOUNG MISSIONARY.

SCARCE was the joyance o'er
  That hail'd the nuptial rite,
And scarce the tender, parting tear
  Dried in its channels bright,
When o'er the Atlantic surge,
  There came a sound of woe,—
The flower that erst our garden deck'd
  Was in its bloom laid low.

Sweet friend—within our souls,
  How fresh each hallow'd trace,
Thy meek forgetfulness of self,
  Thy loveliness and grace,
Thy land, the harp that rul'd,
  Thy warbled music sweet,
Thy childhood's early choice to sit
  Low at thy Saviour's feet.

Within the house of God
  There was a marriage train,
A gather'd throng, a breathless hush,
  An anthem's thrilling strain,
And thou in snowy robe
  Wert by thy lover's side,
While there a hallow'd voice invok'd
  Heaven's blessing on the bride.

Thy path was o'er the wave,
  To ancient climes afar,
Where turns the pagan's blinded eye,
  From Bethlem's blessed star;

But soon, life's labor o'er,
  Thine was a peaceful sleep,
Where richly breathes the Moslem rose,
  And dew-eyed myrtles weep.

And now there's grief for thee,
  Fair inmate of the grave,
Where bright Bosphorus proudly flows,
  And Asia's palm-trees wave,
While deep within *his* soul
  Is anguish unexprest,
Who held thee for so brief a space,
  A pearldrop on his breast.

Not in the churchyard green
  Beneath thy native sky,
Thou by thine infant sister's side,
  Or brother dear might lie,
But with their spirits pure
  Thou join'st a glorious train,
Where ne'er a golden link was broke
  From love's eternal chain.

Sad is thy parent's home,
  And lone their evening-fire,
Yet there doth blessed Memory bend
  And holy hope aspire,
As angel comforters
  They point desponding love
To what thou *wert* while here below,
  And what thou *art* above.

"BLESSED ARE THE PURE IN HEART."

How beautiful the pure in heart go up
To meet their God.
The Spoiler hath his will,
Or seems to have, upon the moveless pulse,
And marble eye-lid. Yet, the victor-palm
Is in His hand, the ever strong to save,
Who waits to crown them as they reach the goal,
Their race well run.
And thus it was with her,
Who at the birth of this cold, wintry morn,
Laid down the burdens of mortality,
The placid beauty of an earlier day
Still linger'd round her features; and her eye
With its deep, loving lustre spoke of peace
That the world could not give. Even in her hours
Of dark bereavement, ne'er a doubt had stolen
Between her heart and Him who chastened it,
But making still His holy will her own,
She gather'd joy from sorrow.
Many a friend
Will miss the warmth of hospitality,
That ever in her ancient mansion glow'd,
And many a sigh from lonely dwellings rise
For the lost bounties of her liberal hand

To ignorance and want. For she had been
A succorer of many, and her name
Is unto them as a remember'd breath
Born of sweet, summer flowers.
And thus she stood
Clad in the panoply of faith and prayer,
Serenely on the verge of four-score years,
Prompt at her Master's call and ripe for heaven;
Then leaning on the breast of filial love
Sank to unbroken sleep.
How beautiful
The pure in heart go forth to meet their God.

SUDDEN DEATH.

Where are ye,—spirits of the dead?
  That erst with us held converse kind?
Bright o'er our hearts your sunlight shed
  And with strong influence moved the mind?

At morn, with tender smile and word
  Ye cheered us on our devious way,
At eve, we marked, with terror stirred,
  A silent form of rigid clay.

This hour, beside the cheerful hearth
  Or at the household board ye sit,
The next,—dissolve the ties of earth,
  And like the impassive shadow flit.

On your sealed lip, the unfinished phrase
  With trembling agony we trace,
And shudder, as with stony gaze
  Ye shut us from your fond embrace.

We vainly search your viewless track,
  We call,—ye deign us no reply,
We weep, but yet ye turn not back,
  To kiss the teardrop from our eye.

Ye hide from us the robe you wear,
  The path you take, the page you read,
And coldly veil the mansion where
  A strange, mysterious life you lead.

Ah! Why is this! What fault is ours?
  That coldly thus, ye haste away,
And heed no more the once lov'd flowers
  That in your pulseless hand we lay?

Heed not the piercing sighs that swell
  From the lone hearts untold despair,
And leave to those ye loved so well
  The load of undivided care.

Oh! spirits of the viewless dead!
  If nought within this world of pain
May hope to lure your backward tread,
  To earth's sweet intercourse again,

Yet bend and teach us not to mourn,
  Unfold the hovering wing, and show
How at one rush the nerves were torn,
  That bind so close to joys below.

We knelt beside your shrouded clay,
  To move with prayers the close seal'd ear,
And now the self-same words we say
  Beside the grave that yawns so drear.

It closes! Must we homeward go,
  The desert-void of life to try?
And miss, amid our toil and woe
  The solace of your love-lit eye?

Bereaved and shelterless and lone,
  There yet remains one place of trust,
The footstool of our Father's throne,
  The humble lip, laid low in dust.

There let us cling though tempest-tost,
  There let us breathe the contrite prayer,
Till, Spirits of the loved and lost!
  Like you, an unknown flight we dare;

From orb to orb,—from sphere to sphere
  Shall what your eyes behold, discern,
What your purg'd ear hath heard, shall hear,
  And what your thoughts conceive, shall learn.

And if, like you, with lowly zeal
  This dim probation path we trod,
Shall at your side enraptured kneel
  Amid the paradise of God.

THE BABE WHO LOVED MUSIC.

THERE was an infant, fair as light,
  With eye of heavenly blue,
A sudden cloud enwrapp'd the scene,
And paleness o'er his placid mein
  Diffus'd a deathlike hue.

So, now, no more his eager feet
  Close to the harp shall pass,
Nor to the sweetly measur'd chime
His little hand keep perfect time
  In playful tenderness.

But doubtless in that better clime
  Where none have shed the tear,
Where discord mars no music strain,
The soul of melody shall gain
  Its own congenial sphere.

THE PASTOR.

Pastor! thou from us art taken,
In the glory of thy years,
As the oak, by tempests shaken
Falls, ere time its glory sears.

Here, where oft thy lip hath taught us
Of the Lamb who died to save,
Where thy guiding hand hath brought us
To the blest baptismal wave,

Pale and cold, we see thee lying
In the temple once so dear,
While the mourner's bitter sighing
Falls unheeded on thine ear.

All thy love and zeal to lead us
Where celestial fountains shine,
And on living bread to feed us,
In our faithful hearts we shrine.

May thy pure example guide us,
Be thy glorious hope our shield,
And the Saviour stand beside us,
When like thee, to Death we yield.

ARTIST SKETCHING THE DEAD.

How still and fair!
'Tis beautiful to trace
Those chisel'd features. Blessed gift is thine
Oh Artist! thus to foil the grave, and keep
A copy of our jewels, when it steals
And locks them from us.
Blessed gift is thine!
And yet how solemn is the privilege
To hold such vigil o'er their brows, who know
Such mysteries as none may learn and live.

—Dost falter, Artist? happy skill is thine!
Give fullness to that lip, which Pain's long kiss,
Hath wasted. And for that pale, Parian cheek
Throw colors on thy pallet, like the rose;
Not the deep damask, but the maiden-blush
Tender, yet frail and tremulous, as love,
Or pity touch'd the heart.
For the soft eyes,
Mix the fresh violet hue. Alas! alas!
There was a shadow o'er them, when they bent
Thro' their long fringes, o'er some hallowed page,
—A light, when on the face of friend they gaz'd,—
A merry sparkle at the touch of mirth.—
Thy pencil fails in all. Dip it once more,

I know not in what dies. Yet try once more.
—Dost ask me of her smile ?
It came from Heaven.
And thou art blameless, if thy mortal hand
Fail to interpret what hath homeward soar'd,
To its own sphere again.
Be patient, friends!
Ask not too much of man. Ye have within
Her finish'd picture. In your heart of hearts
It glows unchang'd. And ye shall know it well
When at Heaven's gate ye see it, fill'd with life
That cannot die.

MOURNING FOR THE AGED.

Why say ye,—when the aged die,
  And find a couch in mouldering clay,
That lightly parts the loosen'd tie,
  And scarcely mourn'd they pass away?

Speak.—ye, who o'er their calm decline
  Have bent so tenderly and long,
Did Love without a pang resign
  Its charge, and seek the unsadden'd throng?

Speak,—ye, who by a father's side
  So fondly watch'd while years swept by,
Making his hoary locks your pride,
  And learning how the righteous die,

Who studious culled from storied page
  Sweets, o'er the deafened ear to strew,
And quicken'd oft the homeward step,
  Because that dim eye watched for you,

Who felt his trusting, helpless age,
  Relying where it once controll'd,
Wake in your soul a thrill that made
  The love of prosperous seasons cold.

Speak! was the shaft of anguish slight,
 And soon dispell'd the painful gloom,
When sank your counselor and guide
 A tenant of the voiceless tomb?

Hence with the thought! It is not so!
 Methinks a deeper woe should wait,
Their loss, whose rooted virtues show
 The ripeness of a lengthen'd date,

When Wisdom's crown so meekly worn
 Is shrouded 'mid their frosted hair,
And from a younger race withdrawn
 The example they but ill could spare.

Then say not, when the aged die,
 And fade from mortal life away,
That lightly parts affections tie,
 Or brief the tear that dews their clay.

THE TOUCHED BIER.

"He touched the bier."
ST. LUKE.

He touch'd the bier! The bearers stood
Transfix'd, like statues pale,
As rose the dead man from his shroud,—
And chang'd to rapture wild and loud,
Despairing sorrow's wail.

'Twas thus in old Judea's day;
And still, when christian mourners pray,
A hand unseen is on the bier,
A voice arrests affliction's tear,
Not to recall to toil and pain,
The sleeper from his rest again,
Though bow'd with grief may Zion mourn,
A column from her temple torn,
Or Love behold o'er hearth and hall
An everlasting shadow fall,—
Yet not for these—they break the gloom,
Or lift the pall, or rend the tomb,
But token true, they deign to give
That he who dies in Christ, shall live;
And though the grave demand its trust
Of earth to earth, and dust to dust,
Still the *touch'd bier* doth tidings tell
Of deathless joy where angels dwell:
Oh mourner! heed the hand, the voice,
And 'mid thy flowing tears rejoice.

THE ONLY DAUGHTER.

Oh mother! if that cherished form,
  Long to thy soul so dear,
Returns no more, to gild the storm,
  Or check the flowing tear,

If the fond hope that firmer grew
  'Mid changeful joys and fears,
No longer with its sparkling dew
  Must light thy lonely years,

Drink deep of memory's gushing spring,
  For well its brink is drest,
With fragrant plants, whose blosoming
  May soothe thy wounded breast.

Breathe, too, of faith, that richer balm
  Which o'er her spirit shed
A tranquil smile, a sabbath calm,
  In the last hour of dread.

Oh Christian mother! since no more
  The yoke of pain she bears,
Nor shrinking treads this stranger shore
  Beset with thorns and cares,

Give thanks for her eternal health
  For her unclouded day,
Unsullied robes, unrusting wealth,
  That cannot fleet away.

And in that dear Redeemer's love
Which none shall trust in vain,
Take refuge, till in heaven above
Thou meet'st thine own again.

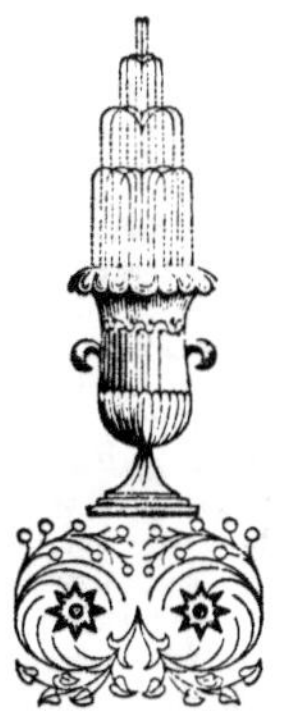

THE FATED BARQUE.

The wreck of the steamer Swallow, on the Hudson river, Monday night, April 7th, 1845.

THE boat pursued her way.
The vernal night
Grew chill with wintry storm, and darkness hung
Dense o'er the waters. Still, that boat pursued
Her venturous course o'er Hudson's troubled tide.

A throng was in her bosom. And anon,
As darkness deepened, and untimely snow
Came strangely drifting through the ebon cloud,
Friends nearer drew, and many a gather'd group
Close seated in the fair saloon, beguiled
The time with sweet discourse.
But all at once
A crash! a rending shock! that prostrate threw
The strongest; while in quick succession came
Like earthquake throes, the horrible response
Of rock to wrecking boat. A rush of steam,
The last pulsation of her broken heart,
Went fiercely up, amid the startling peal
Of human voices, wild with agony.

See! see! the volumed flame, the frantic crowd,
Parents from children torn, and friend from friend,
Swept by the rushing billows, some to die,
And some to reach the barques that doubtful steer

'Mid blast, and tempest, and bewildering gloom,
Intent on rescue. See! on fragments snatched
In haste, yon reckless swimmer dares the flood,
And disappears, while woman's tender form
Maintains a brief death-struggle with the will
Of the fierce waters.
One there was, whose hand
Had placed the last rose in the bridal wreath
About to crown her temples. Fancy drew,
A moment since, bright visions o'er her mind,
In which one manly image foremost shone,—
The expecting lover. What awaits her now?
A fearful conflict with the rugged rock,
The struggle of a moment, and the plunge
That hath no rising here.
There was a pair,
Who held a reckless balance o'er the wave
Upon a frail settee. A lonely child,
Upheld by its white night-dress, floated near,
And clasped the lady's neck, dreaming, perchance,
'Twas his own mother. But no fond embrace
Detained the form that silently went down
To the cold depths.
She, who with yearning heart
Would fain have died to save him, shuddering hung
Upon her husband's arm, who grasped the wreck
Above the whelming breakers. Half submerged,
They strove with the Destroyer, face to face,
Until a voice of mercy bade them live,
When hope receded.

But their noble boy,
Their beautiful, their only one, so late
Laid by a mother's hand to peaceful sleep,
In that lost boat, let them not ask for him,
Since there can be no answer in this world
To such a question, save what hopeless grief
Gives to the smitten spirit.
God of strength!
Who in all time of trouble art our stay,
Thou wilt remember the insensate forms
That sleep beneath the flood, and those who weep
The lorn heart's buried jewels, thou wilt make
Thy path of mystery plain, in the clear light
Of yon unclouded clime.

THE GOOD SON.

Beyond the crested wave,
  In a green island-glade,
Where tropic flowers in beauty bloom,
  His foreign grave is made,

Who in his native clime,
  From youth's unfolding day,
Was still a widow'd mother's hope,
  Her solace, and her stay.

Around, where'er she turns,
  Are trophies of his care,
The tree he set, the vine he train'd,
  The home he made so fair,

His tender accents still
  Like treasur'd music flow,
And memories of the parting prayer
  Shed sunshine o'er her woe.

Yet hence with hopeless grief!
  For one whose path below,
With filial piety sublime,
  And heavenly peace did glow;

For hath he not attain'd
  A clime of blest repose,
A mansion whence is no remove,
  A life no death that knows?

Doth not a beckoning hand
  The mourner's step incite,
To that blest home, where ties of love
  Eternally unite

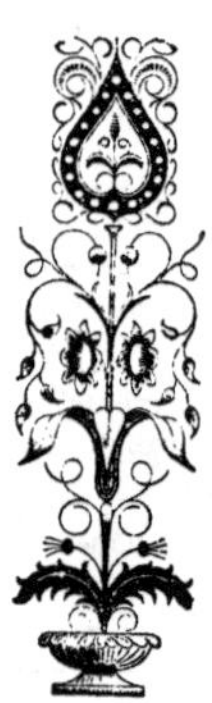

MY FATHER'S STAFF.

THE staff of my father! so trusty and tried,
It bringeth him back to his seat by my side,
Even more than yon picture, with likeness so true,
It bringeth him back, all unchang'd to my view.

It bringeth him back, with his spirit so meek,
The smile and the color still fresh on his cheek;
Good seed had he sown, ere his youth spread the wing,
And the fruitage it bore, made his winter like spring.

He had stood for his land, when the war-cloud was rife,
And in the cool hush of the evening of life,
That staff was his partner, whenever he rov'd
'Mid the plants he had rear'd, or the kindred he lov'd.

Perchance on its head he more heavily prest,
When four-score and eight mark'd their date on his breast;
Yet I know not, indeed, with such vigor he past,
And his step was so buoyant and firm to the last.

The staff of my father! each slow rolling year
Made its friendship more priz'd, and its presence more dear,
He grasp'd it one morn, 'neath the clear, sunny sky,
But resign'd it, alas! ere the twilight, *to die.*

Let it stand! let it stand! where he plac'd it with care,
On the quiet hearth-stone, by his favorite arm-chair,
Let it stand while I live, unmolested and free;
The staff of that blest one is precious to me.

Another he had, and its strength did not fail,
As he trod the dark depths of the shadowy vale,
The staff of his Saviour! That prop may I know,
When through the same vale a lone pilgrim I go.

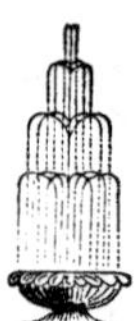

FRIENDSHIP IN SORROW.

TOGETHER, 'neath the early morn,
We took our joyous way,
When clustering blossoms hid the thorn,
And all around was gay,
And now, when midnight's wildest storms,
The troubled sleeper wake,
And fear unveils its phantom form,
Shall I thy side forsake?

Together, when the Spring was new,
From hill, and glen, and bower,
Still arm in arm, we swept the dew,
And cull'd the frequent flower,
And now when Winter's wrath is high.
And vales their robes regret,
And leafless forests quake and sigh,
Shall I thy love forget?

Together, in our blooming age
To Music's realm we turn'd,
Or bending o'er the lesson'd page
The same sweet descant learn'd,
And now, when Time that teacher stern,
Instructs thee how to moan,
Shall I to bowers of pleasure turn
And leave thee sad and lone?

Ah no! beneath misfortune's dart,
  Thy cheek bedew'd with tears,
Thou 'rt dearer to my yearning heart,
  Than even in cloudless years;
For friendship born of prosperous hours
  May have a sparkling eye,
But that which lives when sorrow lowers,
  Claims kindred with the sky.

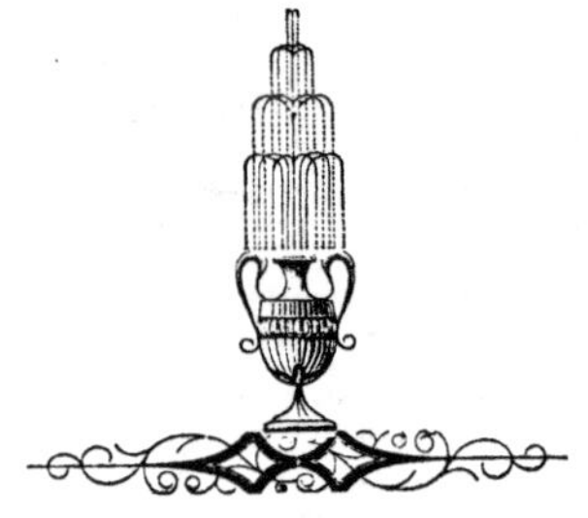

THE EARLY FLED.

Music and flowers, the heaven-born and the fair
  Thou loved'st, and hast fled where neither fade,
Where neither die; and where no cloud shall dare
  The noontide of thy happiness invade;

Too early fled! ah weeper say'st thou so?
  Was it too early from all sin to part?
Or 'scape those shafts of agonizing woe
  That rankle in the loitering pilgrim's heart?

Love droopeth for its loss. But as for thee,
  Faith lifts a song, and o'er thy place of sleep
The tender flowret blooming timidly,
  Doth of thy loveliness meet record keep;

Sweet friend, a sweet farewell! till at the feet
Of thy Redeemer dear, the mourn'd and mourner
    meet.

THE MOURNING WIFE.

"Fair flowing river, and dark, wood-crown'd heights,
That gird so close my solitary home,
What say ye unto me?
There's many a tone
Upon that murmuring tide, when fitful winds
Sweep o'er its bosom; and amid the boughs
That bend above it, many a warbling voice
Floats on the breeze. But to mine ear they speak
Only of one, of him who taught my heart
Amid these mountain-solitudes to taste
Pure love's true happiness.
I bless thee,—stream!
And ye,—cool groves, that keep his image fresh
Thus in your faithful hearts, and speak of him
In your most tender whispers, while I muse
Alone and drooping, where so oft we rov'd
Soul knit to soul, at twilight's hallow'd hour.

And lo! the same sad season comes again,
That bore him from me. With what shuddering grief
Dark memories wake. Away! I may not dwell
On scenes like these.

High hostages he left
With me at parting. O'er the sorrowing breast
Of his beloved parent-guides, to pour
The balm of consolation, and for God
Train up the darling infant-group, that bear
His impress, and his name. Such words he spake
With his pale lips, while loosening my embrace,
He upward hasted, to return no more.

Husband! I'll keep thy charge, while life is mine!
A noble charge, enough to nerve my soul
To tireless labor, and undying hope."

'Twas thus at day's decline, a tender strain
Burst varied forth. At first, it seem'd to sigh
As when the lonely Philomel bemoans
Her sole companion, 'neath the archer's shaft
Laid low. But then, with loftier melody
It caught the dialect of Woman's love,
When in its widow'd self-abandonment
Pouring its life-blood into other hearts,
It seeks no solace, save in duty's task,
And heaven's re-union.

CHRISTIAN TEARS.

"Jesus wept."
ST. JOHN.
"He beheld the city, and wept over it."
ST. LUKE.

CHECK not the tear that flows
  From the heart's inmost core,
When the dear idols of thy love
  Part, to return no more.

For if thy Maker's hand
  Ordain affliction's shock
Why should'st thou seal the stream He bade
  Flow from the smitten rock?

Scorn not the sweet relief,
  Oh man of strength and power!
But freely let the cloud of grief
  Distil its healing shower.

Had it been shame to weep,
  Would *He*, our perfect guide,
Beside the mournful tomb have pour'd
  The sympathetic tide?

Or o'er that City's bound
  Where His pure blood was spilt,
Send forth those precious, pitying drops
  That goodness sheds for guilt?

Check not the holy tear,
But o'er the lifeless clay,
And for the wandering child of sin,
Give Nature's impulse way.

THE STATESMAN.

A VOICE was in the lofty halls
Where meet the wise and great,
And long the listener's ear enchain'd
With eloquent debate.

The voice of one who e'er maintain'd
High thought, and noble deed,
Was in its vigor lifted up
Still for the right to plead.

There came a pause! That voice no more
Sustain'd a nation's trust,
But from the open grave, there rose
A whisper "*dust to dust;*"

A wail of sorrow from a home
Where sweet affections dwell,
While silence settled round the hearth
Where erst his accents fell.

Oh deep shall smitten love deplore
This whelming stroke of fate,
And patriot virtue pensive weep
The unforgotten great.

BABY-BOY TO A DEPARTED SISTER.

Angel-sister, hovering near me,
While my cradle-rest I take,
Scattering from thy radiant pinions
Dreams that cheer me when I wake,

Thou, from every earthly sorrow
Pass'd with innocence of heart,
I, perchance, have yet to borrow
Manhood's knowledge ere I part.

Tears, they say, are for my shedding,
Yet, life's sunny path looks fair,
Thorns and brambles wait my treading,
But the smile of hope is there.

Wheresoe'er my lot may guide me
On through transient joy or pain,
Sister, hover still beside me,
Till, like thee, my wings I gain.

THE HAPPY DEATH.

THE Sabbath dawn'd, and still upon his couch,
Lay the good man. His breath came heavily,
Nor did his mild eye on this pleasant world
Look forth as wont. There was an inward strife
'Tween the destroying Angel, and the clay.
But the meek soul had disengag'd itself,
From earthly conflict, and on poising wing
Waited the Will divine.
His work was done,
Yea, and well done. Life's duties all discharg'd
Its blessings cherish'd with a grateful heart,
And from its sorrows that unrusting gold
Extracted, which no thief can take away.
His four-score years had cast no chill of frost
Into the tide of sympathy, but still
With a clear judgment and an earnest tone
He counsel'd, or partook of other's cares.
For he had been the menter of the young,
As hoary hairs stole o'er him, and had warn'd
Them of the source from whence his solace came,
In all adversity, and urg'd their feet
To shun the broad and choose the narrow way.
And he had told the Pastor whom he lov'd,
As oft in prayer beside his bed he knelt,

That to the gate of Heaven, the way was clear,
And full of glory. He had warmly prest
The farewell kiss on each beloved brow
With thanks, and words of comfort. The fond group
That long had made his scarcely utter'd wish
A study,—and each patient ministry
Of nursing care, a business and delight,
Now, with a tearful gaze regarded him.
Their work was done,—save o'er the laboring lip
To shed the water-drop, or clasp the hand
That render'd no response. Their work was done,
Save to receive that recompense, which Heaven
Hath promis'd unto filial piety.

The Sabbath hours were number'd. As the clock
Noted their calm departure, lo! the soul
Rode forth, upon that midnight chime,—to God.
Most blessed flight!
For though we ill can spare
Our white-hair'd friends, and tho' they grew more dear
Each added month, yet it were selfish, sure
To hold the ripe sheaf from the Harvester,
Or grudge when He doth gather it with joy
Into his garner.

VISION OF LOVELINESS.

Vision of loveliness and grace,
  But once beheld, yet treasur'd well,
With brow of beauty's softest trace
  And lip of music's magic spell,

Thine image in my heart I wreath'd
  Like pearl in Ocean's secret nook,
While hope a syren promise breath'd
  Again upon those charms to look.

Yet ah, no more ! unless the soul
  That undelusive world attain,
Where seas on seas of knowledge roll,
  And peace and love immortal reign ;

Unless yon glorious heights we climb
  Beyond despair, beyond decay,
Where youth is link'd to joy sublime
  And blossoms ne'er to pass away ;

Where myriad hosts in bright array
  With seraph melody of speech
On Heaven's blest errands speed their way,—
  God grant us grace these heights to reach !

There, ever freed from earthly stain,
  From error's maze, from sorrow's rod,
From power of change, or fear of pain,
  The pure in heart, behold their God.

THE CONSENTING MOTHER.

"I SEE green fields, and glowing flowers;
  I see bright streamlets flow;
Sweet voices call to glorious bowers,
  Dear Mother! let me go."

His cheek grew pale. Had hasting Death
  Dealt the last fatal blow?
List! list! once more that fainting breath,
  "Oh Mother! let me go."

How could her love the soul detain
  That struggled to be free?
Or, leaguing with the tyrant Pain,
  Obstruct its liberty?

"Lord! not my will," she said, "but Thine,"
  And high her darling soar'd,
And from the skies that ever shine
  An angel's descant pour'd.

DEATH OF A SUNDAY-SCHOOL SCHOLAR.

"He gathereth the lambs with his arm and carrieth them in his bosom." ISAIAH.

LAMB! in a clime of verdure,
Thy favour'd lot was cast,
No serpent 'mid thy flow'ry food,
Upon thy fold no blast.

Thine were the crystal fountains,
Thine the unclouded sky,
And 'mid thy sports that star of love,
A play-mate brother's eye.

Approving guides caress'd thee,
Where'er thy footsteps rov'd;
The ear that heard thee bles'd thee,
The eye that saw thee lov'd.

Yet life hath snares and sorrows,
From which no friend can save,
And evils might have throng'd thy path,
Which thou wert weak to brave.

Ane so the Heavenly Shepherd,
Before thine infant charms
Had caught the tinge of care or woe,
Did call thee to his arms;

And though the shadowy valley,
With Death's dark frown was dim,
Light cheer'd the stormy passage,
And thou art safe with Him.

THE MEEK CHRISTIAN.

CALM as the stream, that without ripple glides
On in its course serene, blessing its banks
With fresher verdure, and the humblest plants
Cheering, that on its margin grew, or bend
A drooping leaf to touch its waveless breast,—
Such was her life, who in the ancestral tomb
Is laid, this day, with tears.
And as that stream
Blends all serenely with the ocean-tide,
Unmurmuring, unresisting, undismay'd,
So, did she pass from earth.
Upon her soul
There was no shadow,—from her lip no sigh,—
As well befitteth those who early make,
God's countenance, their light.
Nor pain, nor death,
Nor the disruption of affection's ties,
Close woven round the heart, when life was new
Had power to move her patience, or disturb
Her song of praise.
Oh! saintly and beloved,
The pleasant home is darken'd, where thy smile
Of self-forgetfulness, and meek regard
For other's happiness, and perfect peace,
Returns no more.

Yet hast thou left behind
The living beauty of that Christian faith,
Which was thy strength, and now is thy reward.
So may we keep thy pattern in our heart,
So walk like thee, in our Redeemer's ways,
As not to miss thy mansion in the skies,
When our brief task is done.

LIFE'S PEACEFUL CLOSE.

No more amid his pleasant halls
  The master's form is seen,
On hospitality intent,
  All courteous and serene,

No more amid his gardens fair,
  With lingering step, doth rove,
To muse upon that bounteous Hand
  Which crowns the year with love.

O'er him that change hath past, which comes
  To all of mortal clay,
And full of honors, as of years,
  He calmly pass'd away.

Yet not upon his last decline
  Did pain or anguish frown,
For true affection kept its watch
  Untir'd, till life went down,

Till life went down, like set of sun,
  Amid a cloudless sky,
Its tablet bearing, "*Deeds well done,*
  And hopes that cannot die."

DEATH

OF THE ORIGINAL PROPRIETOR OF MOUNT AUBURN.

FROM Albion's shore, in days of old,
  A good man dar'd the main,
A home within the unplanted wild
  For freedom's sake to gain.

O'er many an acre broad and green
  His earnest ploughshare sped,
And fearless, where the Indian roam'd,
  His mansion rear'd its head.

He, o'er Mount Auburn's fair domain
  Enjoy'd a master's sway,
Which then, with undiscover'd charms,
  In Nature's mantle lay,

Unconscious how a future age
  Its beauty's fame might spread,
When in its consecrated breast
  Should sleep the sacred dead.

The good man train'd a numerous race
  In Wisdom's pleasant way,
So, when the icy hand of death
  Was on his temples gray,

With pious love and reverent grief
  Around his couch they prest,
To treasure up each parting word
  Those pallid lips exprest.

Then, kneeling by the patriarch's side
  They joined with filial tear,
That fervent orison to God
  They never more must hear.

They lifted up the holy psalm
  Which, from their earliest days,
Had mingl'd with the household prayer
  The warmth of chanted praise ;

They lifted up the holy psalm,
  But ere its tender close,
Forth on its high and heavenward wing
  The saintly spirit rose.

There's many a realm, where pomp and pride
  Array the lowly grave,
But glory to that simple land
  Which hath *such* funeral stave,

Which more than might of armed host,
  Or steed to battle driven,
Relieth on the bulwark rear'd
  By souls in league with Heaven.

* Derived from a description of Miss C. F. Orne, herself a descendant of this pious man.

THE LOST NEIGHBOR.

THE pure and lovely spirit hath gone home,
Blessing and bless'd.
There was a thrill of pain,
Thro' the quick nerves, a weariness that chain'd
The clasic step, and many a sleepless night
Moving the sympathy of kindred hearts,
Ere that fair clay receiv'd the marble tinge,
And on the pleasant imagery of time
The bright eye clos'd.
'Twas sweet to see her here,
Twining with loving tendrils round the prop
That in paternal fondness shelter'd her,
Or thro' her social feelings shedding joy,
And warbling harmony o'er all around,
Or with a saintly patience arm'd, to meet
Her trial hour. It was a Saviour's love
That gave her tender spirit strength to loose
From earth's green shores, so beautiful with spring,
And youth's unclouded morn, and dare alone,
Cold Jordan's icy waters. So, farewell,
Meek follower of our Lord, thus early deem'd
A mate for angels. When we see a brow
Forever beaming with the inward light
Of happiness in duty, and the smile
Of charity to all, or when we hear
A spirit-stirring burst of sacred song,
Instinct with clear and bird-like melody,
We'll think of thee, and be that thought a prayer
So heard in heaven, that we may share thy bliss.

THOU ART NOT HIM.

Written on seeing in the garden of a departed friend, a stranger who at a distance, resembled *him*.

Thou art not him, though light thy tread,
 Thine earnest glance by taste refined,
And though the smile that curls thy lip
 Give promise of an accent kind,
One moment, wrapp'd in wildering gaze
 I scann'd thy form with vision dim,
Yet now, the brief delusion fades,
 Thou art not him, thou art not him.

The Rhododendron's glorious grace
 The tribute of thy praise hath won,
And from its incense-breathing vase
 The peerless Rose of Malmaison,
The white Azalia's polish'd breast,
 The stately Calla's creamy brim,
Thou lov'st his favorite flowers, but still,
 Thou art not him, thou art not him.

When earliest birds, with welcome song
 Return'd their vernal nests to rear,
His heart, like theirs, with music fraught
 Was ever wont to linger here,

And thou art where he oft would muse,
  Beside yon fountain's lilied brim,
Amid the evergreens,—but ah!
  Thou art not him, thou art not him.

Thou art not him. He sleeps in dust,
  While sweet, and faithful to his side,
The flowers he cherish'd, fondly crept,
  And meekly in his coffin died:
We laid him low, when wintry snows
  Adhesive clad the wind-swept limb,
Fair Spring revives, but never more
  The eye of love may gaze on him.

Even so it is, while here we roam,
  Dark clouds involve affection's sky,
These earthly gardens lose their lord,
  And in our grasp, our idols die:
But He, that ever-living Friend,
  Who foil'd for us, the victor grim,
Still whispereth to the mourning soul
  In all its woes, to trust in Him.

TO MOTHERLESS DAUGHTERS.

REMEMBER what *her* voice hath said,
  Who now in dust is laid,
And treasure every loving word
  Like flowers that cannot fade,
And let her counsels be your guide,
  As you in stature grow,
Hers was that wisdom of the skies,
  That draws the sting from woe.

Remember how that lifted eye
  Hath shed the grateful tear;
As rose your lisping, infant prayer
  To seek a Father's ear,
Remember whence her comfort came,
  To whom she look'd for aid,
And early on that mother's God
  Be your affections staid.

Sweet sisters, keep her image bright,
  Forget not all her care,
The smil'd that sooth'd to nightly rest,
  And made your morning fair,
For wheresoe'er, amid the paths
  Of changeful life you rove,
How can you bear a holier spell
  Than such a mother's love?

FUNERAL OF A YOUNG WIFE.

THERE was a sound of mourning in the halls
Where youth and love had built their halcyon nest,
A voice of those who wail their bosom's flower
Cut down in ripen'd fragrance. Stealthily
The robber hath found out thy bower of joy
Young husband, and hath borne that gem away,
Which on the forehead of thine inmost soul
Was worn and worship'd.
A fair infant's voice
Mingleth with thine its dissonance of grief,
Unconscious what that desolation means
Which to its tender bosom entereth.
She, who so late entwin'd her vows with thine,
Passed on before us, as a lovely dream
That tints the musing heart with thoughts of heaven.
Her gentle nature, and the dove-like smile
Of her exceeding beauty, threw a charm
Around her footsteps, as she steadfast trod
The path of duty, truthful and serene.

Among green boughs she knelt at Christmas time,
And took the symbols of her Saviour's love,
Shedding such tears, as those, who bid farewell
Unto God's earthly courts. But when once more

The quiet moon hung out its crescent pure,
She was not of the shadowy people here
Who call themselves the living. She had gone,
Where change and sickness come not.
Once again
I saw her, where she so had longed to be,
Within the hallowed temple. Chant and dirge
Poured their sweet burden, but she heeded not,
Heard not,—for o'er her brow in heavy folds,
And o'er her form, was laid the sable pall,
Death's bridal veil.
The holy psalmist's words
Who walking lonely through the darkened vale
Did fear no evil, gave a blessed theme
Of consolation unto those who mourned
That solemn hour.
So then, the weepers rose
And took the silent dead, and bare her forth
Unto her wintry couch. But on the snows
That wreathed her pillow, Faith unblenching stood,
And of the resurrection, and the life
That hath no end, spake, and assured the hearts
That sorrowing, left their dearest treasure there.

THE SAILOR'S DYING CHILD.

Dear mother, sit beside my bed,
  And of my father tell,
On the deep ocean far away,
  Where foaming billows swell;
I wish that he were with us now,
  While sick and faint I lie,
'Twere good to hear his loving voice,
  And bless him ere I die.

Mother, it troubles me to see
  Those stranger-ladies come,
And urge you so to leave my side,
  And work for them at home;
Methinks they coldly gaze on me,
  And shake their heads and say,
How feeble and how pale I grow,
  And waste, and waste away.

And oh, it grieves my heart to think,
  From morn to evening shade,
That you so oft for them must toil,
  And have from me no aid;

And then with tender words you say,
  You wish it were not so,
But I should have no food or fire,
  Unless you sometimes go.

When slow the sunset fades away,
  And twilight mists appear,
The sound of your returning step
  Is music to my ear;
How happy are those children dear,
  Who on their couch of pain,
Behold a mother always near,
  But still, I'll not complain.

There's nought on earth I love so much,
  As your dear face to see,
And now, indeed, the time is short
  We can together be;
Still draw me closer to your side,
  And to your bosom fold,
For then my cough I do not heed,
  Nor feel the winter's cold.

Yet when the storm is loud and wild,
  I cover up my head,
And pray Almighty God to save,
  My father from the dead;
So, in his lonely midnight watch
  Upon the tossing sea,
Perhaps beneath the solemn stars
  He will remember me.

I know I cannot see him more,
  I feel it must be so,
But he can find my little grave,
  Where early spring flowers blow;
And you will comfort all his cares,
  When I in heaven shall be;
But mother, dearest! when I die,
  Oh! be alone with me.

THE WISE CHOICE.

"She hath chosen the better part."

In every duty kind and dear
  Whose unobtrusive round
Doth bless the lov'd domestic sphere
  Her chief delight she found.

Still o'er her children's budding minds,
  With gentle zeal to pour
The manna of that word divine
  Which fed the saints of yore.

And when she heard the suffering plaint
  Of penury and care,
Or those who by the wayside faint
  In shelterless despair.

She turn'd not from their sad request,
  Nor scorn'd the tale of grief,
But promptly, with a feeling breast,
  Gave pity and relief.

And doubt ye not, her heavenward trust,
  The path she firmly trod,
Her meek regard for others good,
  And for the Church of God.

The blessing of the grateful poor,
And sorrow's lowly train,
When earth and sea have fled away,
A better crown shall gain,

Than that which dipp'd in gorgeous dies
The world, with loud acclaim
Doth for its favor'd votaries weave,
And proudly christen, *Fame.*

DEATH OF A CLERGYMAN'S BRIDE.

High hopes were form'd for thee, bride of his heart,
Who to God's temple consecrate, did vow
A life-long service. Thy young hand in his,
Thy truthful heart partaker of his joys
And sorrows, and thy strong and spiritual mind
A fervent sharer in his hallow'd toils,
A double strength was his, to "occupy
Until his lord should come."*
High hopes were thine,
To whom the vista of this opening life
Seem'd bright with bloom.
And how have they been crowned!
Ask of the Master, who, with solemn voice,
So early called thee; ask the angel train
To whom thou art a sister; for the eye
Of man hath never seen, nor his dull ear
Heard, nor his earthly heart conceiv'd the bliss
That waits the ransom'd soul.
Thy place below,
At hearth and board is vacant, and the void
In many a tender bosom marks thy loss,
In characters of pain: but Faith doth tell
Of an eternal banquet, and a bond
That never more is sunder'd.

* The text of the funeral sermon.

So, look up,
Ye grieving ones, and when ye think of her,
Give thanks, even while ye weep.
It were not meet
To murmur at her glory, nor desire
To pluck her downward to time's ills again.
Clay mourns for clay, but spirit soars to catch
Some glimpse or sparkle of their glorious joy
Who wear the robes of immortality,
And by such blessed token shapes its course
More truly toward the skies.

THE FATHER TO MOTHERLESS CHILDREN.

Come, gather closer by my side,
  My little smitten flock,
And I will tell of him who brought
  Pure water from the rock,

Who boldly led God's people forth
  From Egypt's wrath and guile,
And once a cradled babe did float
  All helpless on the Nile.

You're weary, precious ones, your eyes
  Are wandering far and wide,
Think ye of her who knew so well
  Your tender thoughts to guide?

Of her who could to wisdom's lore
  Your fixed attention claim?
Ah! never from your hearts erase
  That blessed mother's name.

'Tis time to sing your evening hymn,
  My youngest infant dove,
Come press your velvet cheek to mine,
  And learn the lay of love;

My sheltering arm shall clasp you all,
My poor deserted throng,
Cling as you used to cling to her,
Who sings the angel's song.

Begin, sweet birds, the accustom'd strain,
Come, warble loud and clear,
Alas! alas! you're weeping all,
You're sobbing in my ear.

Good night! go say the prayer she taught
Beside your little bed,
The lips that us'd to bless you there
Are silent with the dead.

A father's hand your course may guide
Amid the thorns of life,
His care protect those shrinking plants
That dread the storms of strife;

But who, upon your infant hearts,
Shall like that mother write?
Who touch the strings that rule the soul?
Dear, smitten flock, good night!

THE BENEVOLENT MAN.

AT sunset's golden close
  We roam'd till dews were shed
Where fair in solemn beauty rose
  The city of the dead,
Its bowers of woven shade,
  And sculptur'd fanes disclose
Where throngs on turf-wrought pillow laid,
  Unconsciously repose.

Though oft that verdant place
  The mourner's feet have trod,
They left behind no frenzied trace,
  To mar the burial sod.
And the flower that lingereth near,
  Refrains the tale to tell
Of sorrow's wildly gushing tear
  That o'er its bosom fell.

Whose is yon new-made grave,
  Where yet no blossoms grow ?
Answer, ye creeping boughs that wave
  As summer breezes blow ;
And the earth murmur'd in her heart,
  And the trees above our head,
Of him who set them both apart*
  Unto the sacred dead.

* The munificent giver of the ground for the cemetry.

Who slumbereth where the sod
  Upon its broken breast
Reveals the recent steps that trod
  Around its hallow'd rest?
And distant tones replied
  Where want and woe are bred,
"He, who reliev'd us when we sigh'd,
  And when we hunger'd, fed."

What trophy will ye raise
  To him who sleeps below,
Who won of righteous men the praise,
  And the grateful prayer from woe?
Hark! to a voice of love
  From yon celestial sphere;
"His deeds are register'd above,
  His full reward is *here*."

CHILD AT THE MOTHER'S GRAVE.

My mother's grave! 'Tis there beneath the trees,
I love to go alone, and sit and think,
Upon that grassy mound. My cradle hours
Come back again so sweetly, when I woke
And lifted up my head, to kiss the cheek
That bow'd to meet me.
And I seem to feel
Once more, the hand that smooth'd my clustering curls,
And led me to the garden, pointing out
Each fragrant flower and bud, or drawing back
My foot, lest I should careless crush the worm
That crawl'd beside me.
And that gentle tone
Teaching to pat the house-dog, and be kind
To the poor cat, and spare the little flies
Upon the window, and divide my bread
With those that hungered, and bow meekly down
To the gray-headed man, and look with love
On all whom God had made.
And then her hymn
At early evening, when I went to rest,
And folded closely to her bosom, sat
Joining my cheek to hers, and pouring out
My broken music, with her tuneful strain:

Comes it not back again,—that holy hymn,
Even now upon my ear?
                    But when I go
To my lone bed, and find no mother there,
And weeping, kneel to say the prayer she taught,
Or when I read the Bible that she lov'd,
Or to her vacant seat at church draw near,
And think of her, a voice is in my heart
Bidding me early seek my God, and love,
My blessed Saviour.
                    Sure, that voice is hers.
I know it is, because these were the words
She used to speak so tenderly, with tears
At the still twilight hour, or when we walked
Forth in the Spring amid rejoicing birds,
Or whispering talked beside the winter fire.

Mother! I'll keep these precepts in my heart,
And do thy bidding.
                    Then, when God shall say
My days are finished, will He give me leave
To come to thee? And can I find thy home,
And see thee with thy glorious garments on,
And kneel at the Redeemer's feet, and beg
That where the mother is, the child may dwell?

THE VICTORY.

On his last rising morn he gaz'd
  With calm and gentle eye,
He bless'd its glad, reviving beam
  But sought a brighter sky.

Out on the fair, empurpled hills
  And where the waters meet,
And gliding, kiss the velvet vales,
  He look'd with memories sweet.

And thus a kind farewell he took
  Of earth in beauty drest,
Bound to a far, returnless borne,
  No unreluctant guest.

Then, meekly in his favorite chair
  Reclin'd with listening ear,
And brow uprais'd, and folded hands,
  The Master's call to hear.

And ever, as with muffled step
  The Spoiler nearer drew,
The holy smile of conquering faith,
  More fix'd, more tranquil grew.

With fatal aim, his shaft he sped,
  And still'd the pulses leap,
But wondering, saw the marble brow
  That smile of victory keep ;

Again, the fount of breath he stanch'd
  And fill'd with ice the veins,
But heard the unharm'd spirit sing
  Amid ethereal plains.

THE BROTHERS.

THE rose of June was fresh and fair,
  The morning sun was bright,
As from their pleasant home they turn'd,
  Replete with young delight,
Beneath a kindred roof to play,
  And cheer affection's eye.
Yet little thought these beauteous boys
  They journey'd there, *to die.*

All joyous fled the shining hours,
  In childhood's pastime dear,
Sweet sports of innocence and love
  That knew, nor care, nor fear,
But sudden as the archer's bow
  Bereaves the warbling nest,
The burning fever's deadly shaft
  Stood rankling in their breast.

Sad change came o'er each polish'd brow,
  And so, we say, *they died,*
Yet rather let us say they rose
  To their Redeemer's side,
To Him, of whom their infant lips
  Would lisp, in tuneful praise,
With cherubim and seraphim
  A higher hymn they raise.

No jarring discord mars the lay,
  No blast the bud shall blight
Where walk the ransom'd of the Cross,
  In garments ever white,
And though the tear of earthly love
  Doth gush in speechless pain,
God grant its alchimy may prove
  The soul's eternal gain.

THE ONLY CHILD.

I SAW the wrinkled and care-written brows
Of the gold-seekers,—and the throngs intent
On idle pleasure,—and the youthful bands
Who gathering round their teachers, wisely sought
The gifts of science, or the arts that lend
Embellishment to life.
Yet, one there was,
One lonely teacher, in her quiet home,
Who taught the harder lesson, *how to die.*
Gentle and fair she was,—the only child
Of loving parents, and had early sate
At her Redeemer's feet, and learn'd his word.
Hence, gain'd her pallid lip such eloquence
That fired the lustrous eye with holier light
As of the joy she spake that fills the soul
When earth recedes, and how her blessed Lord
Seem'd ever near to comfort her, when pain
Wrought at her heart, and how the shadowy vale
Glow'd with his guiding presence.
Messages
For absent friends, and warnings to the young
To seek their Saviour, ere the day of gloom,
She wrapp'd in tender words, more precious still
For their faint breath, that show'd with gasp and sigh,
The time was short.

Yet, one long week she sate
In the cold arms of death, and told what peace
The trusting christian hath,—when flesh and heart
Fail.
Then was silence, for her work was done,
And with a smile that on the marble brow
Like silent angel, finish'd what she left
Unsaid, she clos'd her lesson how to die.
What said we? *how to die?* Nay,—*how to live!*
To enter on a being without end,
A boundless bliss, unutter'd, unconceiv'd.

Oh beautiful and glorious, thou art gone
Unto the lov'd and perfect, who embrac'd
Thee at Heaven's gate. Still, dost thou backward
turn
Beckoning the tender parent guides who liv'd
Here, in thy life ;--and oft, at hush of eve,
Or in the wakeful midnight hour, thy voice
Shall speak to them, when none beside may hear
Sweet words, to gird them on their way to thee.

DEATH OF AN INFANT.

Sweet bud! whose brief perfume
  So cheer'd the parent's breast,
Here, in this grassy tomb
  Enjoy unbroken rest.
Sleep! free from thorn and strife,
  Safe from the Spoiler's rod,
Germ of eternal life
  Sown in the lowly sod.

Sown with baptismal dew
  Fresh on thy folded bloom,
In Christ's strong name and true,
  Go, bide the day of doom.
How will thy perfect flower
  Delight affection's eye,
In yon celestial bower
  Where every tear is dry.

For though the spot be lone
  Where thy bright blossom sprang,
And each remember'd tone
  But wake the parent's pang,
Still let their souls be strong
  God's wisdom to adore,
And join that holy song
  Which thou in heaven dost pour.

THE YOUNG MOTHER.

OH! lovely as the lily's gem
  That 'neath the morning's genial ray,
Uprising on its graceful stem
  Doth meekly greet the King of Day,
I saw thee first, when knowledge won
  Admittance to the unfolding mind,
When all its leaflets toward the sun
  Aspir'd, in purity refined.

But hear I now an infant's wail
  Forc'd from thy sheltering arms to part?
And mark his brow with anguish pale
  Who held thee nearest to his heart?
And can it be, that thou art fled
  To the cold grave, so young and fair?
While scarce the bridal wreath was dead
  That trembled 'mid thy sunny hair?

Fled? ere the dewdrop, bright and fleet,
  Might from thy budding hopes exhale?
Ere of young bliss the carol sweet
  Had pall'd upon the summer gale?
Yet was a strange and glorious power
  To thy departing spirit given,
To smile 'mid terrors darkest hour
  And triumph at the gate of Heaven.

SISTER AT THE BROTHER'S GRAVE.

She stood beside the marble of the dead,
The gifted man, and good.
Tears had their course,
For he who slumbered there, had been to her
The pleasant playmate of her infant years,
And on through manhood and its failing prime,
The hallow'd fountain of that kindred love
Had never known decay.
Tears had their course,
As tender memory from the scenes of old
Once glowing in full plentitude of joy,
Brought the crush'd water-vase, and wither'd wreath
To her, who in that solitary place
Mourn'd o'er departed days.
At length her head
She rais'd from its long drooping, and behold,
What glorious change!
The setting sun had burst
From clouds, and o'er their misty curtains pour'd
A flood of splendor,—crimson blent with gold,
Saffron, and rose, and ruby—fading soft
Into the far serene.—
The very foes
That cast strong shadows o'er his path, were made

New heralds of his glory. So the soul
Fill'd with God's light, doth leave the ills of time,
Regarding not the mockery of their dream
When it awaketh.
                    Nature seem'd to say
"Such was *his* parting whom thou fain hadst held
Longer in bonds of clay."
                    Then, full of joy,
That lonely sister utter'd words of praise,
For in her heart there was a whisper'd sound,
"Such shall thy rising be, if thou wilt cling
Fast to a Saviour's robe."
                    She knew the voice
Of Faith, the seraph, and with added strength
Turn'd from her brother's pillow, leaving there
A weight of grief, and bearing in her hand
A flower from Heaven.

THE TWIN BABES.

TWIN rose-buds crush'd! How sad to see
  Their radiant beauty fled,
And Love's most tender ministry
  Unheeded round their bed,
And Sorrow's melancholy hue
Shading the spot where erst they grew.

Twin harps destroy'd! We say 't is so,
  But err we not the while?
Methought I heard a cadence low
  At day's departing smile,
As though an angel stoop'd to say
Heaven's message to the sons of clay:

"Twin cherubs came to our embrace,
  Our white-rob'd host they join,
They gaze upon the Saviour's face,
  And taste of bliss divine,
While still with voices sweetly strong
They join our everlasting song."

THE LOST POET.

Up to the Spirit-land! the unfinish'd song
Still on thy lip, the breathing lyre
Warm in thy skillful hand,
A spell-bound throng
Intently listening to its thrilling wire;
Thus early call'd by the unerring Sire,
Up to the Spirit-land!

Up to the Spirit-land! thy soul inwrought
To harmony that nought could move,
Not earth's dense atmosphere, nor jarring thought,
Nor the crush'd vase of love,
Scarce could they weave one thread of mournful dye
Into thy woof of song,
For sunbeams kiss'd it from the sky,
Till finely blent and healthfully,
Its colors moved along.

Up to the Spirit-land!
Though we thy music ill can spare,
That charmed away our care.
Up! up! for she is there
O'er whom thy breaking heart-strings rang,
Whose image linger'd till thy latest pang;
She gives to thee her angel hand,

Go, minstrel go!
Though well we love to hear thy numbers flow,
Though still we need
In thy pure life to read
The example of a truthful soul,
Calm in its own communing with the skies,
We, o'er whose heads the sand-clouds roll
The sirochs of our desert way,
Whelming us, when we fain would rise
To wake the living lay!
Yet, minstrel, go!
To thy divine employ;
Leave us to mourn, Earth's lot is woe,
And Heaven's is joy.

THE AGED COMMUNICANT.

God's house was her delight. And thence she drew,
As sabbath after sabbath held their course,
Strength for life's duties, and a lifted heart
To bear its ills. Her's was the spirit-smile
Which age quench'd not, and on her quiet home,
And on the partner of her early days,
And on her children, as they gather'd round,
To the third generation, still she shed
The never-clouded sunbeam of a soul
Enlighten'd from above.
Age hath no chill,
Where the fresh fountain of true charity
Runs with free course. The cheek may take a tinge
From blighting time, but the full nourish'd heart
Weareth no wrinkle.
Thus it was with her;
And Death's deep shadow on her eyelids hung
Briefly. An inward readiness was there
That foil'd his pride.
One sabbath in God's courts
She sate, with healthful and delighted brow,
Sharing the manna-shower,—the next,—a form
Pale and pall-covered, through those aisles was borne,

And laid beside the altar, while the voice
Of one she lov'd, in solemn funeral rite,
Spake of the body in dishonor sown,
Terrestrial and corruptible;

But she,
No more a manna-gatherer here below,
Partook the food of angels.

THE BLESSED TRANSITION.

Scarce on her cherish'd flowers
  Sere Autumn's hand was laid,
Nor curling leaf, nor withering bud
  Its ministry betray'd,
But an earnest eye, she rais'd on high
  Where the blossom cannot fade.

Love had not wan'd, or pal'd,
  Fast by her hearth it grew,
With healthful root, as when it drank
  The earliest morning dew,
Yet she sought sublime, a purer clime,
  For a Saviour's love she knew.

Peace, with a holy veil
  Inwrapp'd her inmost thought,
Foiling the ceaseless shafts of pain
  That still for victory sought,
So, scarce was hush'd the prayer that gush'd,
  Ere an angel's praise she caught.

THE FAIR CHILD.

O BEAUTY! from a mother's arms
  By sudden suffering torn,
And on an earthy pillow laid
  Until the rising morn,

O Innocence! removed before
  The selfish world broke in,
To stain thy tablet, or imprint
  The imagery of sin,

O ties of Love! in anguish rent,
  How hard it were to bear
Such agony of smitten hope
  And unrequited care,

Save for the promise of our Lord
  The sleeper to restore,
And twine again those severed hearts
  Where they can part no more;

Save for the teaching of His love,
  That sorrow's tear shall aid,
The joyous reaping in the skies,
  Where blossoms never fade.

THE MOTHER'S DEPARTURE.

In the fresh morning of her years,
She kiss'd away her nursling's tears,
And laid him, bright with opening charms
Soft, in her mournful daughters arms.

Pain prob'd her breast with fearful pang,
Like breaking lute the heart-strings rang,
Yet Peace, that of her soul was part,
Look'd thro' her eye, and foil'd the dart
Of dark despair,
And wip'd away the deathful dew,
And fann'd the cheek of pallid hue,
With breath of prayer.

On a high arm,—and strong,
The soul its burden cast,
Till soaring free and high
The weakness of mortality
Fled like a wither'd leaf before the rushing blast,
And with a conqueror's song
Heaven's gate she pass'd.

DEATH OF THE FIRST-BORN BABE.

It is not in a land of storms,
 That the fragile plant may grow,
The summer woodbine shrinks away
 When wintry tempests blow,

And is it not in cloudless climes,
 In gardens of the blest,
That the pure blossom of the soul
 Doth find its perfect rest?

So, if the flow'ret thou didst nurse
 All delicate and dear,
Is shelter'd thus,—Oh Mother! spare
 The unavailing tear;

For hop'st thou not, when earthly fear
 And pain shall pass away,
The welcome of thy babe to hear,
 Wrapp'd in an angel's lay?

THE LOST FRIEND.*

Among the noblest of our land, there sprang
A child of beauty, whose unfolding grace
And gentleness of spirit, well repaid
Parental love and prayer.
Her flowing curls
Were of the sunbeam's paly gold, her lip
Gave speech like music, and her fairy tread
Was as the summer-breeze among the flowers.
Though ripening youth, and intellectual lore
Shed heighten'd lustre o'er her eye, and woke
An admiration that might well excite
The flush of vanity, yet graver thought
And early wisdom, well the balance held,
And foil'd the danger.
When maturer years
Brought higher duties, with what pure resolve,
And motives chasten'd by God's holy fear
She took her portion of life's mingled cup,
He best can tell, who walk'd so many years
With her in closest union, mourning now
In the heart's utter loneliness, a loss
That earth can ne'er restore.

* Written on the death of Mrs. Faith Wadsworth, October 19th, 1846.

With dignity
Her matron part she bore, accounting still
Nothing beneath her notice, that pertain'd
To woman's sphere, touching the humblest springs
Of order and of happiness that made
Her hospitable home so beautiful,
And teaching by example, how to mark
With varied industry, each fleeting hour.

High-bred, and graceful, as if train'd in courts,
Yet gentle to the lowliest child of need,
And winning ardent and enduring love
From those who serv'd her, so she held her course,
Making her household, and her own sweet life
Alike a model. Simple and sincere,
No forms of fashion mov'd her to uphold
The artificial, or repress the true.
Yet while with social intercourse she blent
The charm of intellect, or wak'd at will
With playful humor the impulsive smile,
Or press'd the heaven-born precept, nought was
done
From ostentation, or for praise of man;
Humility, that hath the praise of God
Enrob'd her soul.
Judgment was hers, to choose
Best means for wisest ends, and speak right words,
At fitting times. Hers was the power to do
Unpleasant duties kindly, and in love
So wrap reproof, that without sting it wrought
Its chastening office.

Skill'd was she to unwind
The maze of character, and read aright
The intricate, or misinterpreted;
Yet in the foible or the fault she saw
Never to lose the virtue they might shade,
Nor the thrice-blessed charity, that lifts
The trembling motive to the fostering beam
Throwing a mantle o'er those darker ills
It fail'd to heal.
The casting out of self
Left larger room for sympathy, and still
For others good forgetful of her own,
She labor'd with a smile that spoke of heaven.
Hers was the soul for friendship, firm and kind,
Confiding frankly, and with sacred care
Guarding entrusted confidence, unaw'd
At painful service, and in sympathy
So true and tender, that anothers joys
And sorrows seem'd her own, yet pointing still
O'er time's low scenes, to that celestial band
Who fold their wings around us, lest we dash
Our foot against a stone.
For she, than they
Was scarcely lower, and did seem to us
More like an angel-presence shrin'd in clay,
Than one who shar'd in our infirmities.
So felt the poor and sorrowful, who sought
Her aid, or counsel.
But we may not tell
Of her unresting alms-deeds, for she strove
To veil them with such hallow'd secresy,

That even the sufferer might not know from
whence
The balm-drops came, that cheer'd him.
Warm with love
Her bounty in its blessed ministry
Through many a noiseless channel wrought its
way,
Shunning all trace, save what it could not shun,
A daily record in the Book of Heaven.

But now her pleasant mansion, fair with all
That taste could give, is desolate.
The chair
Is vacant, where so oft we saw her sit,
Her form unbow'd by time, and brow inspir'd
With that peculiar beauty of the skies
Which saintly age doth wear.
To yonder room
Of blest retirement, with those chosen guests,
The ever-studied Bible, and the page
Of sacred meditation, where she went
With every rising and retiring day,
Her step returns no more.
Each in its place
There are her garments as she laid them down
With her own gentle hand, as at the close
Of that last sabbath evening, to her couch
With words of earnest, trusting prayer, she came,
And whence her ready spirit rose serene
Ere breaking dawn.
We may not hope to look
Upon her like again.

But praise to Him
Who lent the jewel to us, and in love
Hath taken it to himself,undimm'd, unharm'd
By earth's attrition.
Be the wisdom ours
So in our hearts some blessed trait to keep
Of her example, that we may not lose
The teachings of her life, or of our tears.—
For well we know, the ever-living root
Of all her goodness, was a piety
Humble and self-abas'd before its God,
Yet in its stewardship to man, so just,
So full of love, as not to need a change
Even for yon realm of love, save that which marks
Bright morn advancing toward the Perfect Day.

THE LOT OF EARTH.

THERE 's mourning 'mid the boughs,
High in the forest fair,
The widow'd linnet wails her spouse,
Caught in the fowler's snare;

While the forsaken nest
Laments with shriller woe,
The gentle robin's brooding breast,
Pierced by the archer's bow.

There 's mourning 'mid the flocks
That graze the verdant plain,
When from the yearning mother's side
The playful lamb is slain.

There 's mourning in the flood,
For what the barbed hook
And the wide-spread, unpitying net
In sweeping vengeance took,

And where the dire harpoon
Doth the vex'd wave distain,
And with strong agony transfix
The monarch of the main.

There 's mourning in the field,
The grass that fell to-day,
Reluctant, to the scythe did yield
Its fragrant life away.

And the reaper in his path,
  How little doth he heed
The expiring of the mangled swathe
  That at his feet doth bleed!

The maiden, as she goes
  Among the flowers at morn,
Recks not the weeping of the rose
  That from its bud is torn.

Though mourning all around,
  In ocean, earth, and air,
Doth tell that grief-seeds sow the ground,
  And blossom every where:

But man's aspiring race,
  Who in their pilgrim path
Must oft the mocking phantom chase,
  And drink the cup of wrath,

With unrepining heart
  This discipline should share,
And to the heaven appointed dart
  The breast in silence bare,

Since they alone, of all
  Creation's sorrowing train,
May hope these fleeting ills shall work
  Their everlasting gain.

www.ingramcontent.com/pod-product-compliance
Lightning Source LLC
LaVergne TN
LVHW021420110826
845150LV00007B/2012

* 9 7 8 1 4 2 5 5 0 8 7 7 7 *